INTRODUCTION

Welcome to 33 Super Healthy Honey [Dessert Recipes], your guide to creating mouthwatering, honey-infused [desserts that are as delicious] as they are nourishing! Whether you're [looking to satisfy your sweet] tooth guilt-free, impress at your next gathering, or explore the magic of honey as nature's sweetener, this collection is here to inspire you.

Each recipe has been carefully crafted using wholesome ingredients and naturally sweetened with honey, ensuring every bite is packed with flavor, nutrients, and health benefits. From luscious cakes to decadent puddings, you'll discover desserts that satisfy your cravings while supporting your wellness goals.

We'd love to see how you get creative with these recipes! Make sure to follow us on Instagram at @health.base33 (https://instagram.com/health.base33) for daily health tips, inspiration, and updates. When you make your own honey-infused creations from this book, don't forget to tag us—we'd love to feature your desserts on our page and share them with our growing community! It's a fun way to inspire others, showcase your unique take on these recipes, and celebrate the joy of healthy living together.

At 33 Super Healthy Honey Dessert Recipes, we believe in the power of community and the magic of creating together. Sharing your creations spreads the joy of healthy living and encourages others to join in on the delicious fun.

By tagging @health.base33 (https://instagram.com/health.base33) in your posts, you'll have the chance to be featured on our page and inspire countless dessert lovers. We can't wait to see how you personalize these recipes and bring your creative flair to each dish!

Lastly, if you've enjoyed this recipe book, we'd be so grateful if you could leave a 5-star review on Amazon. Your feedback helps others discover these delicious honey-infused recipes and supports our mission of spreading health and happiness. Thank you for being a part of our honey-loving community, and don't forget to share your creations on Instagram and leave a review to let others know how much you love these sweet and healthy treats!

1. Honey Almond Flour Brownies
2. Honey Lavender Panna Cotta
3. Honey Pistachio Baklava Bites
4. Honey Coconut Macaroons
5. Honey Peach Cobbler
6. Honey Chia Seed Pudding with Fresh Berries
7. Honey-Glazed Almond Flour Donuts
8. Honey Blueberry Greek Yogurt Parfait
9. Honey Lemon Poppy Seed Muffins
10. Honey Almond Granola Clusters
11. Honey-Baked Cinnamon Apples with Almond Crumble
12. Honey Tahini Bliss Balls
13. Honey Matcha Coconut Truffles
14. Honey Lemon Thyme Cheesecake Bars
15. Honey Rose Pistachio Mousse
16. Honey Carrot Cake Bites with Cream Cheese Drizzle
17. Honey Mocha Tiramisu
18. Honey Strawberry Shortcake
19. Honey Almond Cream Tart with Fresh Berries
20. Honey Mango Coconut Pudding
21. Honey Cashew Butter Blondies
22. Honey Raspberry Swirl Cheesecake Bars
23. Honey Lemon Poppy Seed Bundt Cake
24. Honey Cardamom Pear Tarts
25. Honey Orange Blossom Panna Cotta
26. Honey Matcha Cheesecake Bars
27. Honey Chocolate Avocado Mousse
28. Honey Citrus Yogurt Parfait
29. Honey Tahini Swirl Brownies
30. Honey-Glazed Pear Galette with Almond Crust
31. Honey Matcha Eclairs
32. Honey Almond Crème Brûlée
33. Honey Cinnamon Swirl Bread Pudding

Once you've created your delicious recipe, **share it with us** on Amazon and leave a review! Simply scan this QR code to get started.

Check out our other healthy recipe cookbooks for more delicious inspiration!

33 Super Healthy Air Fryer Recipes

33 Super Healthy Ice Cream Recipes

33 Super Healthy Vegan Dessert Recipes

33 Super Healthy Keto Dessert Recipes

HONEY ALMOND FLOUR BROWNIES

These Honey Almond Flour Brownies are a deliciously healthy alternative to traditional brownies. Sweetened naturally with honey and made with almond flour, they're packed with protein, healthy fats, and rich chocolate flavor, making them an indulgent yet guilt-free treat.

Serves: 9
Prep Time: 15 minutes
Cook Time: 25 minutes

Ingredients

- 1 ½ cups almond flour
- ½ cup unsweetened cocoa powder
- ½ teaspoon baking powder
- ¼ teaspoon salt
- 3 large eggs
- ½ cup honey
- ¼ cup coconut oil (melted)
- 1 teaspoon vanilla extract
- ½ cup dark chocolate chips (optional, for added richness)

Instructions

1. Preheat Oven:
- Preheat your oven to 350°F (175°C).
- Line an 8x8-inch baking pan with parchment paper.

2. Mix Dry Ingredients:
- In a large bowl, whisk together almond flour, cocoa powder, baking powder, and salt.

3. Combine Wet Ingredients:
- In a separate bowl, beat the eggs.
- Add honey, melted coconut oil, and vanilla extract. Mix well.

4. Create Batter:
- Gradually fold the wet ingredients into the dry mixture.
- Stir until well combined and smooth. If using, fold in the dark chocolate chips.

5. Transfer to Pan:
- Pour the batter into the prepared baking pan and spread evenly.

6. Bake:
- Bake for 25–30 minutes or until a toothpick inserted into the center comes out clean.
- Allow the brownies to cool completely in the pan before slicing into squares.

HONEY LAVENDER PANNA COTTA

This dessert is a perfect balance of creamy and floral, using honey as a natural sweetener and lavender to provide calming properties. The recipe is dairy-free and low in processed sugars, making it a guilt-free treat.

Serves: 6
Prep Time: 15 minutes
Cook Time: 4 hours (chill time)

Ingredients

- 1 cup full-fat coconut milk
- 1 cup unsweetened almond milk
- 1/4 cup honey
- 1 1/2 teaspoons dried culinary lavender
- 1 1/2 teaspoons unflavored gelatin powder
- 2 tablespoons cold water
- 1/2 teaspoon vanilla extract
- Fresh berries and honey drizzle for topping (optional)

Instructions

1 Prepare Lavender Infusion:
- In a small saucepan, combine the coconut milk (or cream) with honey and dried lavender.
- Heat over medium-low heat, stirring occasionally, for about 5 minutes until hot (but not boiling).
- Remove from heat, cover, and let the lavender infuse for 10 minutes.

2 Bloom the Gelatin:
- While the lavender is steeping, sprinkle the gelatin over 3 tablespoons of cold water in a small bowl.
- Let it sit for 5 minutes to bloom.

3 Strain and Dissolve:
- Strain the lavender mixture through a fine mesh sieve to remove the buds, then return it to the saucepan.
- Reheat gently and stir in the bloomed gelatin until fully dissolved.

4 Add Vanilla:
- Remove from heat and stir in the vanilla extract.

5 Pour and Chill:
- Divide the mixture evenly among 4 small ramekins or glasses.
- Cover with plastic wrap and refrigerate for at least 4 hours, or until set.

6 Garnish and Serve:
- Before serving, garnish with fresh lavender sprigs, a drizzle of honey, and optional almonds or berries.

HONEY PISTACHIO BAKLAVA BITES

This dessert transforms the classic baklava into bite-sized portions, using honey as the primary sweetener and pistachios for their heart-healthy fats. The result is a perfectly crunchy, nutty treat that satisfies your sweet tooth without refined sugar.

Serves: 12
Prep Time: 20 minutes
Cook Time: 25 minutes

Ingredients

- 1 cup pistachios, finely chopped
- 1/2 cup almonds, finely chopped
- 1 teaspoon ground cinnamon
- 8 sheets of phyllo dough
- 1/4 cup melted coconut oil
- 1/3 cup honey

Instructions

1 Prepare Nut Mixture:
- Combine the chopped pistachios, almonds, and cinnamon in a small bowl.

2 Layer Phyllo Dough:
- Place one sheet of phyllo dough on a clean surface and lightly brush with melted coconut oil.
- Layer another sheet on top and repeat until all eight sheets are stacked.

3 Cut and Fill:
- Cut the phyllo stack into 12 squares.
- Place a teaspoon of the nut mixture in the center of each square.
- Fold the edges inward to create small parcels.

4 Bake:
- Arrange the parcels on a baking sheet lined with parchment paper.
- Bake at 350°F (175°C) for 20–25 minutes, or until golden brown.

5 Add Honey:
- Drizzle honey over the warm baklava bites as soon as they come out of the oven.
- Let them cool and absorb the honey before serving.

HONEY COCONUT MACAROONS

These Honey Coconut Macaroons are a delightful blend of chewy coconut and natural sweetness from honey. Free from refined sugars, they provide a wholesome and satisfying treat perfect for a guilt-free indulgence.

Serves: 20
Prep Time: 15 minutes
Cook Time: 20 minutes

Ingredients

- 3 cups unsweetened shredded coconut
- 1/2 cup raw honey
- 1/2 teaspoon vanilla extract
- 2 large egg whites
- 1/4 teaspoon sea salt

Instructions

1. Prepare the Pan:
- Preheat your oven to 350°F (175°C).
- Grease an 8-inch square baking pan with coconut oil or line it with parchment paper for easy removal.

2. Make the Coconut Base:
- In a large bowl, combine the almond flour, shredded coconut, and salt.
- Add the melted coconut oil and honey, stirring until the mixture resembles wet sand.

3. Form the Base:
- Press the coconut mixture evenly into the prepared baking pan.
- Use the back of a spoon or a flat spatula to smooth the surface.

4. Bake the Base:
- Place the pan in the preheated oven and bake for 10–12 minutes, or until the edges are lightly golden.

5. Prepare the Honey Drizzle:
- While the base bakes, mix honey, vanilla extract, and a pinch of sea salt in a small bowl.

6. Drizzle and Cool:
- Once the base is baked, remove it from the oven and drizzle the honey mixture evenly over the top.
- Allow the bars to cool completely in the pan before slicing into squares.
- Once cooled, cut into 12 squares.

HONEY PEACH COBBLER

This Honey Peach Cobbler combines the natural sweetness of ripe peaches with a touch of honey for a guilt-free indulgence. It's made with whole-grain oats and almond flour for added fiber and nutrients, making it a delicious and wholesome dessert.

Serves: 6
Prep Time: 15 minutes
Cook Time: 40 minutes

Ingredients

- 6 ripe peaches, peeled, pitted, and sliced
- 1/4 cup honey
- 1 tablespoon lemon juice
- 1 teaspoon cinnamon
- 1/2 teaspoon vanilla extract

Topping:
- 1 cup almond flour
- 1/2 cup rolled oats
- 1/4 cup melted coconut oil
- 2 tablespoons honey
- 1/4 teaspoon baking soda
- Pinch of salt

Instructions

1 Prepare the Filling:
- Preheat your oven to 375°F (190°C).
- In a large mixing bowl, combine the peach slices, honey, lemon juice, cinnamon, and vanilla extract.
- Mix well to coat the peaches evenly.

2 Assemble the Filling:
- Pour the peach mixture into an 8x8-inch baking dish and spread it evenly.

3 Prepare the Topping:
- In another mixing bowl, combine the almond flour, rolled oats, baking soda, and salt.
- Add the melted coconut oil and honey, stirring until the mixture forms a crumbly texture.

4 Add the Topping:
- Sprinkle the crumbly topping evenly over the peaches, covering them completely.

5 Bake:
- Place the baking dish in the preheated oven and bake for 35–40 minutes, or until the topping is golden brown and the peaches are bubbling.

6 Cool and Serve:
- Remove from the oven and let cool for 10 minutes.
- Serve warm, optionally with a dollop of Greek yogurt or a drizzle of additional honey.

HONEY CHIA SEED PUDDING WITH FRESH BERRIES

This Honey Chia Seed Pudding is a powerhouse of nutrients, featuring omega-3-rich chia seeds and the natural sweetness of honey. It's a refreshing, no-cook dessert perfect for a quick and healthy treat.

Serves: 4
Prep Time: 10 minutes
Cook Time: None

Ingredients

- 1/4 cup chia seeds
- 1 1/2 cups unsweetened almond milk
- 3 tablespoons honey
- 1/2 teaspoon vanilla extract
- A pinch of salt
- Fresh berries (strawberries, blueberries, or raspberries) for topping
- Optional garnish: mint leaves

Instructions

1. Prepare the Chia Pudding Base:
- In a medium-sized mixing bowl, whisk together the almond milk, honey, vanilla extract, and a pinch of salt.
- Slowly add the chia seeds while continuously whisking to prevent clumping.

2. Refrigerate:
- Cover the bowl with plastic wrap or transfer the mixture into individual serving jars.
- Refrigerate for at least 4 hours, or overnight, to allow the chia seeds to swell and thicken into a pudding-like consistency.

3. Assemble the Dessert:
- Before serving, give the pudding a good stir to ensure even consistency.
- Top each serving with a generous layer of fresh berries and garnish with mint leaves if desired.

4. Serve:
- Serve chilled as a light and satisfying dessert or snack.

HONEY-GLAZED ALMOND FLOUR DONUTS

These Honey-Glazed Almond Flour Donuts are a guilt-free treat that combines the fluffiness of traditional donuts with the natural sweetness of honey. Packed with protein and low in refined sugars, they make a perfect indulgence without compromising on health.

Serves: 8
Prep Time: 15 minutes
Cook Time: 12 minutes

Ingredients

- 2 cups almond flour
- 1/4 cup coconut flour
- 1 teaspoon baking powder
- 1/2 teaspoon baking soda
- 1/4 teaspoon sea salt
- 2 large eggs
- 1/3 cup unsweetened almond milk
- 1/4 cup honey
- 2 tablespoons melted coconut oil
- 1 teaspoon vanilla extract

For the Glaze:

- 1/4 cup honey
- 2 teaspoons almond milk

Instructions

1 Prepare the Batter:
- Preheat your oven to 350°F (175°C).
- In a medium-sized mixing bowl, combine almond flour, coconut flour, baking powder, baking soda, and sea salt.
- In another bowl, whisk together the eggs, almond milk, honey, melted coconut oil, and vanilla extract until smooth.
- Gradually fold the wet ingredients into the dry mixture, stirring until a thick batter forms.

2 Fill the Donut Pan:
- Lightly grease a donut pan with coconut oil.
- Spoon the batter into the donut molds, filling each one about 3/4 full.

3 Bake:
- Place the pan in the preheated oven and bake for 10–12 minutes, or until the donuts are golden brown and a toothpick inserted comes out clean.
- Let the donuts cool in the pan for 5 minutes before transferring them to a wire rack.

4 Prepare the Glaze:
- In a small saucepan over low heat, warm the honey and almond milk together, stirring until smooth.

Dip the cooled donuts into the glaze, coating the tops evenly.

5 Serve:
- Let the glaze set for a few minutes before serving. Enjoy your healthy donuts with a drizzle of extra honey if desired!

HONEY BLUEBERRY GREEK YOGURT PARFAIT

This parfait combines the natural sweetness of honey with the rich creaminess of Greek yogurt and the antioxidant power of blueberries. It's a guilt-free indulgence perfect for breakfast or dessert.

Serves: 4
Prep Time: 10 minutes
Chill Time: 30 minutes

Ingredients

- 2 cups Greek yogurt (plain, full-fat or low-fat)
- 3 tablespoons raw honey
- 1 teaspoon vanilla extract
- 1 cup fresh blueberries
- 1/2 cup granola (sugar-free or homemade)
- 2 tablespoons chopped almonds or walnuts (optional)

Instructions

1. Prepare Yogurt Base:
- In a mixing bowl, combine Greek yogurt, honey, and vanilla extract.
- Stir well until the mixture is smooth and creamy.

2. Layer the Parfait:
- In serving glasses or jars, add a layer of Greek yogurt mixture to the bottom.
- Top with a layer of fresh blueberries and then a layer of granola.
- Repeat the layers until the glass is full, finishing with a dollop of yogurt on top.

3. Chill and Serve:
- Place the parfaits in the refrigerator for at least 30 minutes to allow the flavors to meld.
- Garnish with additional blueberries and a drizzle of honey before serving.
- Add a sprinkle of chopped nuts, if desired.

HONEY LEMON POPPY SEED MUFFINS

These muffins offer a zesty citrus flavor with a delicate sweetness from honey, providing a refreshing and light treat. The poppy seeds add a delightful crunch and are a source of essential nutrients.

Serves: 12
Prep Time: 15 minutes
Cook Time: 20 minutes

Ingredients

- 1 ¾ cups almond flour
- ¼ cup coconut flour
- 2 tablespoons poppy seeds
- 1 teaspoon baking powder
- ¼ teaspoon baking soda
- ¼ teaspoon salt
- 2 large eggs
- ½ cup honey
- ⅓ cup coconut oil, melted
- ¼ cup almond milk
- 2 tablespoons freshly squeezed lemon juice
- 1 tablespoon lemon zest

Instructions

1 Prepare Dry Ingredients:
- In a medium-sized bowl, whisk together almond flour, coconut flour, poppy seeds, baking powder, baking soda, and salt.
- Set aside.

2 Mix Wet Ingredients:
- In another bowl, whisk the eggs until frothy.
- Add honey, melted coconut oil, almond milk, lemon juice, and lemon zest to the eggs. Mix until smooth and well combined.

3 Combine Wet and Dry Ingredients:
- Gradually add the dry ingredients to the wet mixture.
- Stir gently until just combined, being careful not to overmix.

4 Fill Muffin Pan:
- Line a muffin tin with paper liners.
- Spoon the batter evenly into the prepared liners, filling each about three-quarters full.

5 Bake:
- Preheat the oven to 350°F (175°C).
- Bake the muffins for 18–20 minutes, or until a toothpick inserted into the center comes out clean.

6 Cool and Serve:
- Allow the muffins to cool in the pan for 5 minutes before transferring them to a wire rack.
- Serve warm or at room temperature.

HONEY ALMOND GRANOLA CLUSTERS

Honey Almond Granola Clusters are the perfect guilt-free snack or breakfast topping. Sweetened naturally with honey, these clusters are loaded with heart-healthy almonds and whole oats, providing a fiber-rich and energy-boosting treat.

Serves: 10 (makes about 4 cups)
Prep Time: 10 minutes
Cook Time: 25 minutes

Ingredients

- 3 cups rolled oats
- 1 cup chopped almonds
- 1/2 cup shredded unsweetened coconut
- 1/3 cup sunflower seeds
- 1/4 cup chia seeds
- 1/2 teaspoon cinnamon
- 1/4 teaspoon salt
- 1/3 cup coconut oil, melted
- 1/3 cup honey
- 1 teaspoon vanilla extract

Instructions

1 Preheat Oven:
- Preheat your oven to 325°F (160°C) and line a large baking sheet with parchment paper.

2 Combine Dry Ingredients:
- In a large mixing bowl, combine the rolled oats, chopped almonds, shredded coconut, sunflower seeds, chia seeds, cinnamon, and salt.
- Mix well.

3 Prepare Wet Mixture:
- In a small saucepan, melt the coconut oil over low heat.
- Stir in the honey and vanilla extract until well combined.

4 Mix Together:
- Pour the wet mixture over the dry ingredients.
- Stir until all the dry ingredients are evenly coated.

5 Form Clusters:
- Spread the mixture evenly onto the prepared baking sheet.
- Press it down firmly using the back of a spatula to encourage clumping.

6 Bake:
- Bake for 20–25 minutes, or until the granola is golden brown.
- Stir gently halfway through baking to ensure even toasting but try to keep some clusters intact.

7 Cool and Store:
- Let the granola cool completely on the baking sheet—it will crisp up as it cools.
- Break into clusters and store in an airtight container for up to two weeks.

HONEY-BAKED CINNAMON APPLES WITH ALMOND CRUMBLE

A warm and cozy dessert featuring tender baked apples infused with honey and cinnamon, topped with a crunchy almond crumble. This gluten-free, naturally sweetened treat is rich in fiber, healthy fats, and antioxidants, perfect for a guilt-free indulgence!

Serves: 4
Prep Time: 15 minutes
Cook Time: 30 minutes

Ingredients

- 4 medium apples, cored and sliced into 1/4-inch wedges
- 3 tablespoons honey (divided)
- 1 teaspoon ground cinnamon
- 1/2 teaspoon ground nutmeg
- 1 tablespoon lemon juice
- 1/2 cup almond flour
- 1/4 cup rolled oats (gluten-free if needed)
- 1/4 cup sliced almonds
- 2 tablespoons coconut oil (melted)
- 1/4 teaspoon vanilla extract
- A pinch of sea salt
- Optional: 1/4 cup plain Greek yogurt (unsweetened) for serving

Instructions

1. Prepare the Apples:
- Preheat your oven to 350°F (175°C). In a large mixing bowl, combine the apple slices, 2 tablespoons of honey, ground cinnamon, ground nutmeg, and lemon juice.
- Toss the apples with a spoon or your hands until they are evenly coated with the honey and spices.
- Transfer the apple mixture to a medium baking dish (about 8x8 inches), spreading the slices out in an even layer.

2. Make the Almond Crumble:
- In a separate medium bowl, combine the almond flour, rolled oats, sliced almonds, melted coconut oil, the remaining 1 tablespoon of honey, vanilla extract, and a pinch of sea salt.
- Stir with a spoon or use your fingers to mix until the ingredients form a crumbly texture, with small clumps forming.
- If the mixture feels too dry, add a teaspoon more of melted coconut oil and mix again.

3. Assemble and Bake:
- Sprinkle the almond crumble mixture evenly over the top of the apples in the baking dish, ensuring all the apples are covered.
- Press down lightly with your fingers to help the crumble adhere to the apples. Place the baking dish in the preheated oven and bake for 30 minutes, or until the apples are tender and the crumble topping is golden brown and crisp.
- Check the apples with a fork to ensure they're soft; if needed, bake for an additional 5 minutes.

4. Serve:
- Remove the baked apples from the oven and let them cool for 5 minutes to set. Divide the warm dessert into four serving bowls or plates. For an extra touch of creaminess, add a dollop of plain Greek yogurt (about 1 tablespoon per serving) on top of each portion, if desired.
- Drizzle with a tiny bit of extra honey (about 1/2 teaspoon per serving) for a glossy finish. Serve immediately to enjoy the warm, comforting flavors, pairing with a cup of herbal tea for a cozy experience

HONEY TAHINI BLISS BALLS

These Honey Tahini Bliss Balls are an excellent source of plant-based protein, healthy fats, and natural sweetness. They make the perfect energy-boosting snack or guilt-free dessert to enjoy any time of the day.

Serves: 12
Prep Time: 15 minutes
Cook Time: None

Ingredients

- 1 cup rolled oats
- 1/2 cup tahini
- 1/4 cup honey
- 1/4 cup almond flour
- 1/4 cup unsweetened shredded coconut
- 1/4 cup dark chocolate chips
- 1 teaspoon vanilla extract
- 1/2 teaspoon ground cinnamon
- Pinch of sea salt
- Extra shredded coconut for rolling (optional)

Instructions

1 Prepare the Mixture:
- In a large mixing bowl, combine the rolled oats, tahini, honey, almond flour, shredded coconut, dark chocolate chips, vanilla extract, ground cinnamon, and a pinch of sea salt.
- Mix well until all ingredients are evenly incorporated and form a sticky dough.

2 Form the Balls:
- Scoop out about a tablespoon of the mixture and roll it into a ball between your hands.
- Repeat until all the mixture is used, making approximately 12 balls.

3 Coat (Optional):
- If desired, roll the balls in extra shredded coconut for an added layer of texture and flavor.

4 Chill:
- Place the bliss balls on a plate or tray and refrigerate for at least 20 minutes to firm up.

5 Serve:
- Enjoy the Honey Tahini Bliss Balls as a snack or dessert. Store any leftovers in an airtight container in the refrigerator for up to one week.

HONEY MATCHA COCONUT TRUFFLES

These Honey Matcha Coconut Truffles are a perfect balance of sweet and earthy flavors, offering a healthy energy boost with the antioxidants of matcha. The natural sweetness from honey makes them a guilt-free indulgence, perfect for snacking or as a dessert.

Serves: 12
Prep Time: 20 minutes
Chill Time: 30 minutes

Ingredients

- 1 cup shredded unsweetened coconut
- 2 tablespoons matcha powder
- 3 tablespoons raw honey
- 1/4 cup almond flour
- 2 tablespoons melted coconut oil
- 1/2 teaspoon vanilla extract

Instructions

1 **Prepare the Mixture:**
- In a medium bowl, combine the shredded coconut, matcha powder, and almond flour.
- Stir in the melted coconut oil, honey, and vanilla extract until the mixture is sticky and well combined.

2 **Shape the Truffles:**
- Scoop out tablespoon-sized portions of the mixture.
- Roll each portion into a smooth ball using your hands.

3 **Chill the Truffles:**
- Place the truffles on a plate lined with parchment paper.
- Refrigerate for at least 30 minutes to set.

4 **Serve:**
- Once firm, transfer the truffles to an airtight container.
- Store them in the fridge for up to a week and enjoy as a quick, healthy treat.

HONEY LEMON THYME CHEESECAKE BARS

This delightful dessert combines the tangy zest of lemon, the herbal touch of thyme, and the natural sweetness of honey for a healthier take on a classic cheesecake. Made with a nut-based crust and a creamy honey-sweetened filling, these bars are as nutritious as they are indulgent.

Serves: 12
Prep Time: 25 minutes
Cook Time: 35 minutes

Ingredients

For the Crust:

- 1 ½ cups almond flour
- ¼ cup coconut oil, melted
- 3 tbsp honey
- 1 tsp vanilla extract
- Pinch of salt

For the Filling:

- 2 cups cream cheese (room temperature)
- ½ cup Greek yogurt
- ⅓ cup honey
- Zest and juice of 2 lemons
- 1 tsp vanilla extract
- 1 tsp fresh thyme leaves (optional)
- 2 large eggs

Instructions

1. Prepare the Crust:
- Preheat your oven to 325°F (160°C).
- In a medium bowl, combine the almond flour, melted coconut oil, honey, vanilla extract, and salt. Mix until the mixture resembles wet sand.
- Press the crust mixture evenly into a parchment-lined 9x9-inch baking dish.
- Bake for 10 minutes, then let it cool while preparing the filling.

2. Prepare the Filling:
- In a large mixing bowl, beat the cream cheese until smooth and creamy.
- Add the Greek yogurt, honey, lemon zest, lemon juice, and vanilla extract. Beat until well combined.
- Stir in the fresh thyme leaves, if using.
- Add the eggs one at a time, mixing well after each addition.

3. Assemble and Bake:
- Pour the filling over the pre-baked crust, spreading it evenly with a spatula.
- Bake for 25 minutes or until the center is just set.
- Remove from the oven and let the cheesecake bars cool to room temperature. Then refrigerate for at least 2 hours.

4. Serve:
- Slice into 12 bars.
- Garnish with a drizzle of honey, a sprinkle of lemon zest, and a sprig of thyme (optional).
- Serve chilled and enjoy!

HONEY ROSE PISTACHIO MOUSSE

This elegant mousse combines the delicate floral notes of rose water with the nuttiness of pistachios, all naturally sweetened with honey. Packed with antioxidants and healthy fats, this dessert is as nutritious as it is luxurious.

Serves: 6
Prep Time: 20 minutes (plus 2 hours chilling)
Cook Time: 0 minutes

Ingredients

- 1 ½ cups unsalted pistachios (shelled and finely ground)
- 1 cup heavy cream (or coconut cream for a dairy-free option)
- 3 tablespoons honey
- 1 teaspoon rose water
- 1 teaspoon vanilla extract
- 2 tablespoons powdered gelatin (or agar-agar for vegetarian option)
- ¼ cup warm water

Instructions

1 Prepare the Gelatin Mixture:
- Dissolve the powdered gelatin in ¼ cup warm water.
- Let it sit for 5 minutes until it blooms.

2 Whip the Cream:
- In a large mixing bowl, beat the heavy cream until soft peaks form.
- Add the honey, rose water, and vanilla extract, and gently fold them into the cream.

3 Add the Gelatin:
- Gently warm the bloomed gelatin mixture in the microwave or over a stovetop until fully dissolved.
- Gradually fold the dissolved gelatin into the whipped cream mixture.

4 Incorporate the Pistachios:
- Carefully fold in the ground pistachios, ensuring they are evenly distributed throughout the mixture.

5 Chill the Mousse:
- Transfer the mixture into serving glasses or a large bowl.
- Refrigerate for at least 2 hours, or until the mousse is set and firm.

6 Garnish and Serve:
- Sprinkle additional ground pistachios on top and add a few rose petals for decoration.
- Serve chilled and enjoy the delightful blend of nutty and floral flavors!

HONEY CARROT CAKE BITES WITH CREAM CHEESE DRIZZLE

These bite-sized Honey Carrot Cake treats are packed with the natural sweetness of honey and the wholesome goodness of carrots. Perfect for satisfying your dessert cravings without compromising on health, these bites are loaded with fiber and nutrients.

Serves: 12
Prep Time: 20 minutes
Cook Time: 15 minutes

Ingredients

For the Cake Bites:

- 1 cup grated carrots
- 1 cup almond flour
- 1/4 cup coconut flour
- 1/4 cup honey
- 1/4 cup coconut oil, melted
- 2 large eggs
- 1/2 teaspoon vanilla extract
- 1/2 teaspoon ground cinnamon
- 1/4 teaspoon ground nutmeg
- 1/4 teaspoon baking soda
- Pinch of salt

For the Drizzle:

- 2 tablespoons cream cheese, softened
- 1 tablespoon honey
- 1 tablespoon unsweetened almond milk

Instructions

1. Prepare the Cake Batter:
- Preheat your oven to 350°F (175°C).
- Line a mini muffin tin with paper liners or lightly grease it with coconut oil.
- In a medium bowl, whisk together the almond flour, coconut flour, baking soda, cinnamon, nutmeg, and salt.
- In another bowl, mix the eggs, honey, melted coconut oil, and vanilla extract until smooth.
- Fold the dry ingredients into the wet ingredients, then add the grated carrots. Mix until evenly combined.

2. Bake the Cake Bites:
- Scoop the batter into the prepared mini muffin tin, filling each cup about 3/4 full.
- Bake for 12–15 minutes, or until a toothpick inserted in the center comes out clean.
- Let the bites cool completely in the tin before transferring them to a wire rack.

3. Prepare the Cream Cheese Drizzle:
- In a small bowl, whisk together the cream cheese, honey, and almond milk until smooth and slightly runny.

4. Assemble and Serve:
- Drizzle the cream cheese mixture over the cooled carrot cake bites.
- Serve immediately or store in an airtight container in the refrigerator for up to 3 days.

HONEY MOCHA TIRAMISU

This Honey Mocha Tiramisu is a lighter take on the classic Italian dessert, made with wholesome ingredients and natural honey for sweetness. The combination of Greek yogurt and mascarpone creates a creamy texture while reducing fat and boosting protein.

Serves: 8
Prep Time: 20 minutes
Chill Time: 4 hours

Ingredients

- 1 cup brewed espresso (cooled)
- 1/4 cup honey
- 1/4 cup unsweetened cocoa powder
- 1/2 teaspoon vanilla extract
- 1 cup mascarpone cheese
- 1 cup Greek yogurt (plain)
- 12 whole-grain ladyfinger cookies
- 1/4 cup dark chocolate (grated, for garnish)

Instructions

1. Prepare Coffee Mixture:
- Brew 1 cup of espresso and let it cool.
- Stir in honey and vanilla extract until well combined.

2. Make the Cream Layer:
- In a mixing bowl, combine mascarpone cheese and Greek yogurt.
- Blend until smooth and creamy.

3. Layer the Dessert:
- Dip each ladyfinger briefly into the honey-espresso mixture.
- Arrange half the soaked ladyfingers in the bottom of a square dish.
- Spread half of the mascarpone mixture evenly over the ladyfingers.
- Dust with unsweetened cocoa powder.

4. Repeat Layers:
- Add another layer of soaked ladyfingers, followed by the remaining mascarpone mixture.
- Dust with another layer of cocoa powder.

5. Chill:
- Cover the dish with plastic wrap and refrigerate for at least 4 hours or overnight to allow the flavors to meld.

6. Garnish and Serve:
- Before serving, sprinkle grated dark chocolate on top for an added touch of decadence.
- Slice and serve chilled.

HONEY STRAWBERRY SHORTCAKE

This Honey Strawberry Shortcake is a healthier twist on the classic dessert. Sweetened only with natural honey and made with wholesome ingredients, it's a perfect balance of flavor and nutrition. The whole wheat biscuits provide fiber, while the fresh strawberries and honey offer a burst of natural sweetness and vitamins.

Serves: 6
Prep Time: 25 minutes
Cook Time: 15 minutes

Ingredients

For the Biscuits:
- 2 cups whole wheat flour
- 1 tablespoon baking powder
- 1/4 teaspoon salt
- 1/4 cup cold unsalted butter, cubed
- 1/4 cup honey
- 2/3 cup unsweetened almond milk

For the Filling:
- 2 cups fresh strawberries, hulled and sliced
- 2 tablespoons honey

For the Whipped Cream:
- 1 cup heavy cream (or coconut cream for dairy-free)
- 2 tablespoons honey
- 1 teaspoon pure vanilla extract

Instructions

1. Prepare the Biscuits:
- Preheat your oven to 400°F (200°C).
- In a large mixing bowl, combine the whole wheat flour, baking powder, and salt.
- Add the cold cubed butter and use a pastry cutter or your fingers to mix until the texture resembles coarse crumbs.
- Stir in the honey and almond milk until a dough forms.
- Turn the dough out onto a lightly floured surface and gently knead it a few times.
- Roll out the dough to about 1-inch thickness and cut into 6 rounds using a biscuit cutter or the rim of a glass.
- Place the biscuits on a parchment-lined baking sheet and bake for 12–15 minutes, or until golden brown.
- Allow the biscuits to cool slightly.

2. Prepare the Strawberries:
- In a bowl, toss the sliced strawberries with 2 tablespoons of honey.
- Let the mixture sit for 10 minutes to macerate the strawberries and create a natural syrup.

3. Make the Whipped Cream:
- In a chilled bowl, whip the heavy cream, honey, and vanilla extract until soft peaks form.
- For a dairy-free option, whip coconut cream instead.

4. Assemble the Shortcakes:
- Slice each biscuit in half horizontally.
- Place the bottom half of a biscuit on a serving plate.
- Spoon a generous amount of the honey-sweetened strawberries onto the biscuit.
- Add a dollop of whipped cream on top of the strawberries.
- Place the top half of the biscuit over the whipped cream and add a final spoonful of strawberries and whipped cream on top for garnish.
- Serve immediately and enjoy this delightful, honey-infused dessert!

HONEY ALMOND CREAM TART WITH FRESH BERRIES

This Honey Almond Cream Tart combines a crunchy almond crust with a luscious honey-infused cream filling and fresh berries. Packed with antioxidants and natural sweetness, it's a guilt-free indulgence that's as stunning as it is delicious.

Serves: 8
Prep Time: 30 minutes
Cook Time: 20 minutes

Ingredients

For the Almond Crust:
- 2 cups almond flour
- 1/4 cup coconut oil, melted
- 2 tbsp honey
- 1/2 tsp vanilla extract
- Pinch of salt

For the Honey Cream Filling:
- 1 cup Greek yogurt (unsweetened)
- 1/2 cup cream cheese, softened
- 1/4 cup honey
- 1 tsp vanilla extract

For the Topping:
- 1 cup fresh strawberries, sliced
- 1/2 cup fresh blueberries
- 1/2 cup fresh raspberries
- 2 tbsp honey (for drizzling)

Instructions

1. Prepare the Crust:
- Preheat your oven to 350°F (175°C).
- In a medium bowl, combine almond flour, melted coconut oil, honey, vanilla extract, and salt.
- Mix until the dough holds together and is slightly crumbly.
- Press the mixture evenly into a 9-inch tart pan with a removable bottom.
- Use your fingers or the back of a spoon to press the crust firmly against the sides and base.
- Bake the crust for 10–12 minutes, or until golden brown.
- Remove from the oven and let it cool completely.

2. Make the Honey Cream Filling:
- In a large bowl, whisk together Greek yogurt, cream cheese, honey, and vanilla extract until smooth and creamy.
- Cover the mixture and refrigerate for at least 15 minutes to firm up.

3. Assemble the Tart:
- Once the crust has cooled, spread the honey cream filling evenly across the tart base.
- Arrange the sliced strawberries, blueberries, and raspberries decoratively on top of the filling.

4. Add the Finishing Touches:
- Drizzle 2 tablespoons of honey over the fresh berries for added sweetness and shine.
- Refrigerate the tart for 1 hour before serving to allow the flavors to meld together.

5. Serve and Enjoy:
- Slice the tart into 8 portions and serve chilled.

HONEY MANGO COCONUT PUDDING

This tropical dessert blends the sweetness of ripe mangoes with the creaminess of coconut milk, naturally sweetened with honey. It's a refreshing and dairy-free treat, rich in vitamins and antioxidants, perfect for hot summer days.

Serves: 4
Prep Time: 10 minutes
Cook Time: 2 hours of chilling)

Ingredients

- 2 ripe mangoes, peeled and diced
- 1 cup coconut milk (full fat)
- 3 tablespoons raw honey
- 1 tablespoon chia seeds
- 1 teaspoon pure vanilla extract
- Optional toppings: shredded coconut, diced mango, mint leaves

Instructions

1 Prepare the Mango Base:
- Peel and dice the ripe mangoes into small pieces.
- Blend the mangoes in a blender until smooth, creating a mango puree.

2 Mix the Pudding:
- In a medium bowl, combine the mango puree, coconut milk, honey, chia seeds, and vanilla extract.
- Stir the mixture thoroughly to ensure the chia seeds are evenly distributed.

3 Chill the Pudding:
- Pour the mixture into serving glasses or bowls.
- Cover each serving with plastic wrap and refrigerate for at least 2 hours, allowing the chia seeds to expand and the pudding to set.

4 Garnish and Serve:
- Before serving, top each pudding with shredded coconut, extra diced mango, and a sprig of mint for a burst of freshness.

HONEY CASHEW BUTTER BLONDIES

These Honey Cashew Butter Blondies are a protein-packed treat that replaces refined sugars with nutrient-rich honey for natural sweetness. Perfect for a guilt-free indulgence, they're made with wholesome ingredients to satisfy your dessert cravings without compromising your health.

Serves: 12
Prep Time: 15 minutes
Cook Time: 25 minutes

Ingredients

- 1 cup cashew butter (unsweetened)
- 2 large eggs
- 1/3 cup raw honey
- 1 tsp pure vanilla extract
- 1/2 tsp baking soda
- 1/4 tsp sea salt
- 1/4 cup dark chocolate chips (optional)
- 1/4 cup chopped cashews (optional, for topping)

Instructions

1 Prepare the Batter:
- In a mixing bowl, combine the cashew butter, eggs, honey, and vanilla extract.
- Mix until smooth and well combined.

2 Add Dry Ingredients:
- Sprinkle in the baking soda and sea salt.
- Fold in the chocolate chips, if using, for an extra indulgent touch.

3 Transfer to Pan:
- Grease an 8x8-inch baking dish or line it with parchment paper.
- Pour the batter into the pan and spread it evenly with a spatula.

4 Add Toppings:
- Sprinkle the chopped cashews over the batter for added crunch, if desired.

5 Bake:
- Preheat your oven to 350°F (175°C).
- Bake the blondies for 20–25 minutes, or until the edges are golden and a toothpick inserted in the center comes out clean.

6 Cool and Slice:
- Let the blondies cool completely in the pan before slicing into 12 squares.

HONEY RASPBERRY SWIRL CHEESECAKE BARS

These Honey Raspberry Swirl Cheesecake Bars are a decadent yet healthy treat, featuring a honey-sweetened cream cheese filling and a naturally vibrant raspberry swirl. Packed with antioxidants from raspberries and the natural sweetness of honey, this dessert is indulgent and wholesome.

Serves: 12
Prep Time: 20 minutes
Cook Time: 35 minutes

Ingredients

For the Crust:

- 1 ½ cups almond flour
- 3 tbsp coconut oil, melted
- 2 tbsp honey
- 1 tsp vanilla extract

For the Raspberry Swirl:

- 1 cup fresh raspberries
- 2 tbsp honey

For the Cheesecake Filling:

- 2 cups cream cheese, softened
- ½ cup Greek yogurt
- ⅓ cup honey
- 2 large eggs
- 1 tsp vanilla extract
- 1 tbsp lemon juice

Instructions

1. Prepare the Crust:
- Preheat the oven to 325°F (160°C) and line an 8x8-inch baking pan with parchment paper.
- In a medium bowl, combine almond flour, melted coconut oil, honey, and vanilla extract. Mix until the texture resembles wet sand.
- Press the mixture firmly into the bottom of the prepared pan, creating an even layer.
- Bake for 10 minutes, then set aside to cool slightly.

2. Prepare the Cheesecake Filling:
- In a large mixing bowl, beat the softened cream cheese and Greek yogurt until smooth and creamy.
- Add honey, eggs, vanilla extract, and lemon juice. Beat until well combined and no lumps remain.

3. Prepare the Raspberry Swirl:
- In a small saucepan, combine raspberries and honey over medium heat.
- Cook for 5–7 minutes, stirring occasionally, until the raspberries break down into a sauce-like consistency.
- Strain through a fine mesh sieve to remove seeds, leaving a smooth raspberry puree.

4. Assemble and Bake:
- Pour the cheesecake filling over the baked crust, spreading evenly with a spatula.
- Drop small dollops of raspberry puree over the filling. Use a toothpick or skewer to swirl the puree into the cheesecake layer, creating a marbled effect.
- Bake for 25 minutes or until the edges are set and the center is slightly jiggly.

5. Cool and Serve:
- Allow the cheesecake to cool completely at room temperature, then refrigerate for at least 4 hours, preferably overnight.
- Once chilled, slice into bars and serve.

HONEY LEMON POPPY SEED BUNDT CAKE

This Honey Lemon Poppy Seed Bundt Cake is bursting with citrusy brightness, perfectly balanced by the nuttiness of almond flour and sweetness of honey. It's gluten-free, refined sugar-free, and provides a delightful dose of healthy fats and antioxidants.

Serves: 10
Prep Time: 20 minutes
Cook Time: 35 minutes

Ingredients

Cake:

- 2 ½ cups almond flour
- ½ cup coconut flour
- 1 ½ teaspoons baking powder
- ½ teaspoon baking soda
- ¼ teaspoon salt
- 3 large eggs
- ⅓ cup melted coconut oil
- ½ cup honey
- 1 tablespoon lemon zest
- ⅓ cup fresh lemon juice
- 1 tablespoon poppy seeds
- ½ cup unsweetened almond milk

Glaze:

- 2 tablespoons honey
- 1 tablespoon fresh lemon juice
- 1 teaspoon lemon zest

Instructions

1. Prepare the Oven and Pan:
- Preheat the oven to 350°F (175°C).
- Grease a bundt pan thoroughly with coconut oil and lightly dust with coconut flour to prevent sticking.

2. Mix Dry Ingredients:
- In a large bowl, whisk together almond flour, coconut flour, baking powder, baking soda, salt, and poppy seeds.
- Set aside.

3. Mix Wet Ingredients:
- In another bowl, beat the eggs.
- Add melted coconut oil, honey, lemon zest, lemon juice, and almond milk. Mix until well combined.

4. Combine Mixtures:
- Gradually add the dry ingredients to the wet ingredients, stirring gently until fully combined.

5. Bake:
- Pour the batter evenly into the prepared bundt pan.
- Smooth the top with a spatula.
- Bake for 35–40 minutes, or until a toothpick inserted into the center comes out clean.

6. Prepare the Glaze:
- While the cake cools, whisk together honey, lemon juice, and lemon zest in a small bowl.

7. Glaze the Cake:
- Once the cake is cooled completely, drizzle the glaze evenly over the top.
- Allow the glaze to soak into the cake before serving.

HONEY CARDAMOM PEAR TARTS

This dessert combines the sweetness of honey with the warm, aromatic flavors of cardamom and cinnamon, creating a delicate balance of taste. With pears providing fiber and nutrients, this tart is both elegant and healthy.

Serves: 6
Prep Time: 25 minutes
Cook Time: 25 minutes

Ingredients

- 1 sheet of puff pastry, thawed
- 2 ripe pears, thinly sliced
- 3 tbsp honey
- 1 tsp ground cardamom
- 1/4 tsp cinnamon
- 2 tbsp almond flour
- 1/4 cup chopped pistachios
- 1 egg, beaten (for egg wash)

Instructions

1. Prepare the Filling:
- In a small bowl, mix the honey, cardamom, and cinnamon until combined.
- Thinly slice the pears and toss them gently in the honey mixture to coat evenly.

2. Prepare the Puff Pastry:
- Preheat the oven to 375°F (190°C) and line a baking sheet with parchment paper.
- Roll out the thawed puff pastry on a lightly floured surface.
- Cut the pastry into six equal squares or rectangles.

3. Assemble the Tarts:
- Sprinkle a pinch of almond flour in the center of each pastry square.
- Layer the honey-coated pear slices neatly on top of the almond flour, leaving a small border around the edges.
- Fold the edges of the pastry slightly over the pears to form a border.

4. Add Toppings:
- Sprinkle chopped pistachios over the pears.
- Brush the edges of the pastry with the beaten egg for a golden finish.

5. Bake:
- Place the tarts on the prepared baking sheet and bake for 20–25 minutes, or until the pastry is puffed and golden brown.

6. Finish and Serve:
- Drizzle a little extra honey over the tarts after baking.
- Serve warm or at room temperature for a delightful treat.

HONEY ORANGE BLOSSOM PANNA COTTA

This luscious panna cotta combines the subtle floral essence of orange blossom with the natural sweetness of honey. It's a refined dessert that is both light and indulgent, made without refined sugar, and perfect for any occasion.

Serves: 6
Prep Time: 15 minutes
Chill Time: 4 hours

Ingredients

- 1 ½ cups unsweetened almond milk
- 1 ½ cups heavy cream or coconut cream
- ¼ cup raw honey
- 2 teaspoons orange blossom water
- 1 packet (2 ½ teaspoons) unflavored gelatin
- 3 tablespoons cold water
- Fresh orange zest and edible flowers for garnish

Instructions

1. Prepare the Gelatin:
- Sprinkle the gelatin over 3 tablespoons of cold water in a small bowl.
- Let it sit for 5-7 minutes to bloom.

2. Heat the Milk Mixture:
- In a medium saucepan, combine the almond milk, heavy cream, and honey.
- Heat the mixture over medium heat, stirring occasionally, until it's hot but not boiling.

3. Incorporate the Gelatin:
- Remove the saucepan from heat and stir in the bloomed gelatin until fully dissolved.
- Add the orange blossom water and mix well.

4. Pour into Molds:
- Divide the mixture evenly into six small ramekins or dessert glasses.
- Let the panna cotta cool slightly before covering with plastic wrap.

5. Chill:
- Refrigerate for at least 4 hours or until set.

6. Garnish and Serve:
- Before serving, top each panna cotta with fresh orange zest and edible flowers.
- Serve chilled and enjoy this elegant treat.

HONEY MATCHA CHEESECAKE BARS

These Honey Matcha Cheesecake Bars are a guilt-free indulgence. The matcha provides a boost of antioxidants, while the honey offers natural sweetness and enhances the rich creaminess of the dessert.

Serves: 8
Prep Time: 20 minutes
Cook Time: 25 minutes

Ingredients

Crust:
- 1 cup almond flour
- 2 tablespoons coconut oil, melted
- 1 tablespoon honey
- Pinch of sea salt

Filling:
- 1 ½ cups Greek yogurt
- 8 ounces cream cheese, softened
- 3 tablespoons honey
- 1 tablespoon matcha powder
- 2 teaspoons vanilla extract
- 1 large egg

Instructions

1 Prepare the Crust:
- Preheat the oven to 350°F (175°C).
- In a mixing bowl, combine almond flour, melted coconut oil, honey, and a pinch of sea salt.
- Mix until the texture resembles wet sand.
- Press the mixture firmly into the bottom of an 8x8-inch baking pan lined with parchment paper.
- Bake the crust for 8–10 minutes, or until lightly golden. Remove and set aside to cool.

2 Prepare the Filling:
- In a large bowl, whisk together the Greek yogurt, softened cream cheese, honey, matcha powder, and vanilla extract until smooth.
- Add the egg and mix gently until incorporated. Avoid overmixing to prevent air bubbles.

3 Assemble and Bake:
- Pour the filling over the cooled crust, spreading it evenly with a spatula.
- Bake in the preheated oven for 20–25 minutes, or until the edges are set and the center slightly jiggles.
- Remove from the oven and let it cool to room temperature, then refrigerate for at least 4 hours or overnight.

4 Serve:
- Cut into squares or bars. Optionally, dust with additional matcha powder for decoration.

HONEY CHOCOLATE AVOCADO MOUSSE

This creamy dessert combines the rich decadence of chocolate with the healthy fats of avocado, naturally sweetened with honey. Packed with antioxidants and heart-healthy nutrients, this mousse is a guilt-free indulgence.

Serves: 4
Prep Time: 15 minutes
Chill Time: 1 hour

Ingredients

- 2 ripe avocados
- 1/4 cup unsweetened cocoa powder
- 1/3 cup raw honey
- 1 teaspoon vanilla extract
- Pinch of sea salt
- 2 tablespoons almond milk (optional, for consistency)

Instructions

1. Prepare the Avocados:
- Cut the avocados in half and remove the pits.
- Scoop the flesh into a blender or food processor.

2. Add the Ingredients:
- Add cocoa powder, honey, vanilla extract, and sea salt to the blender.
- Blend until smooth and creamy, scraping down the sides as needed.

3. Adjust Consistency:
- If the mousse is too thick, add almond milk one tablespoon at a time and blend until you reach the desired consistency.

4. Chill the Mousse:
- Transfer the mousse into serving dishes or ramekins.
- Refrigerate for at least 1 hour to allow the flavors to meld.

5. Serve:
- Garnish with fresh berries, shredded coconut, or a drizzle of honey before serving.

HONEY CITRUS YOGURT PARFAIT

This Honey Citrus Yogurt Parfait offers a refreshing and tangy flavor profile, perfect for a light dessert or snack. Packed with probiotics from yogurt, vitamin C from citrus fruits, and natural sweetness from honey, this dessert is as nutritious as it is delicious.

Serves: 4
Prep Time: 15 minutes
Cook Time: None

Ingredients

- 2 cups Greek yogurt (unsweetened)
- 2 tablespoons honey
- 1 teaspoon vanilla extract
- 1 orange, peeled and segmented
- 1 grapefruit, peeled and segmented
- 1/2 cup granola (optional, for crunch)
- Zest of 1 lemon
- Mint leaves, for garnish

Instructions

1 Prepare the Yogurt Base:
- In a medium bowl, combine the Greek yogurt, honey, and vanilla extract.
- Stir until smooth and well incorporated.

2 Prepare the Citrus Fruits:
- Peel and segment the orange and grapefruit, removing any seeds.
- Cut the segments into bite-sized pieces for easy layering.

3 Assemble the Parfaits:
- Spoon 2 tablespoons of the yogurt mixture into the bottom of a glass or jar.
- Add a layer of orange and grapefruit pieces on top.
- Sprinkle a thin layer of granola (if using) over the fruits.
- Repeat the layers until the glass is full, finishing with a dollop of yogurt on top.

4 Garnish and Serve:
- Sprinkle the lemon zest over the top layer.
- Add a small mint leaf for a fresh finish.
- Serve immediately or refrigerate for up to 2 hours before serving.

HONEY TAHINI SWIRL BROWNIES

These Honey Tahini Swirl Brownies bring a unique twist to classic brownies by incorporating the nutty richness of tahini and the natural sweetness of honey. Packed with antioxidants from dark chocolate and healthy fats from tahini, these brownies are both indulgent and nourishing.

Serves: 9
Prep Time: 15 minutes
Cook Time: 25 minutes

Ingredients

- 1/2 cup honey
- 1/3 cup tahini
- 1/4 cup unsweetened cocoa powder
- 1/2 cup dark chocolate chips (70% cocoa or higher)
- 2 large eggs
- 1/3 cup coconut oil, melted
- 1 teaspoon vanilla extract
- 1/2 cup almond flour
- 1/4 teaspoon baking powder
- 1/4 teaspoon salt

Instructions

1 Prepare the Batter:
- Preheat your oven to 350°F (175°C).
- Line an 8x8-inch baking pan with parchment paper, allowing some overhang for easy removal.
- In a microwave-safe bowl, melt the dark chocolate chips and coconut oil together in 20-second intervals, stirring between each, until smooth.
- Stir in the honey, tahini, eggs, and vanilla extract until fully combined.

2 Mix Dry Ingredients:
- In a separate bowl, whisk together almond flour, cocoa powder, baking powder, and salt.
- Gradually fold the dry ingredients into the wet mixture until just combined.

3 Assemble the Swirls:
- Pour the brownie batter into the prepared baking pan, spreading it evenly with a spatula.
- Drizzle 2 tablespoons of tahini over the batter and use a knife or skewer to create swirls.

4 Bake:
- Bake for 20–25 minutes, or until a toothpick inserted into the center comes out with a few moist crumbs.
- Allow the brownies to cool completely in the pan before slicing into squares.

HONEY-GLAZED PEAR GALETTE WITH ALMOND CRUST

This rustic Honey-Glazed Pear Galette is the perfect blend of natural sweetness and wholesome ingredients. With its almond crust and fresh pear filling, it's a guilt-free treat rich in fiber, healthy fats, and antioxidants.

Serves: 8
Prep Time: 20 minutes
Cook Time: 35 minutes

Ingredients

For the Almond Crust:
- 1 ½ cups almond flour
- 2 tbsp coconut flour
- 2 tbsp honey
- ¼ tsp salt
- 4 tbsp coconut oil (cold)
- 1–2 tbsp cold water

For the Filling:
- 3 medium ripe pears, thinly sliced
- 2 tbsp honey
- 1 tsp ground cinnamon
- 1 tsp vanilla extract
- 1 tbsp almond flour

For the Glaze:
- 2 tbsp honey
- 1 tbsp warm water

Instructions

1. Prepare the Almond Crust:
- Combine almond flour, coconut flour, and salt in a bowl.
- Add cold coconut oil and mix with a fork or hands until crumbly.
- Drizzle in honey and 1 tbsp of cold water, mixing until the dough forms.
- Add another tbsp of water if the dough feels too dry.
- Shape the dough into a ball, wrap in plastic, and refrigerate for 15 minutes.

2. Preheat the Oven:
- Set the oven to 375°F (190°C). Line a baking sheet with parchment paper.

3. Prepare the Filling:
- In a bowl, toss sliced pears with honey, cinnamon, and vanilla extract.
- Sprinkle almond flour over the mixture to absorb excess moisture.

4. Roll the Dough:
- Place the chilled dough between two sheets of parchment paper.
- Roll into a 10-inch circle, about ¼ inch thick.
- Transfer the dough to the prepared baking sheet.

5. Assemble the Galette:
- Arrange the pear slices in the center of the crust, leaving a 2-inch border.
- Gently fold the edges over the pears, pleating as you go, to form a rustic shape.

6. Bake:
- Bake in the preheated oven for 30–35 minutes, or until the crust is golden and the pears are tender.
- Mix honey with warm water and brush over the pears and crust while still warm.
- Let the galette cool for 10 minutes before slicing. Serve warm or at room temperature.

HONEY MATCHA ECLAIRS

This unique dessert combines the earthy flavor of matcha with the natural sweetness of honey, creating a healthier take on the classic éclair. It's packed with antioxidants from the matcha powder and uses wholesome, natural ingredients for a guilt-free indulgence.

Serves: 6
Prep Time: 45 minutes
Cook Time: 25 minutes

Ingredients

For the Choux Pastry:

- 1/2 cup water
- 1/4 cup unsalted butter
- 1/8 tsp sea salt
- 1/2 cup whole wheat pastry flour
- 2 large eggs

For the Matcha Honey Filling:

- 1 cup Greek yogurt (full-fat or 2%)
- 3 tbsp honey
- 2 tsp matcha powder

For the Honey Glaze:

- 2 tbsp honey
- 1 tbsp matcha powder (for dusting)

Instructions

1. Prepare Choux Pastry:
- Preheat your oven to 375°F (190°C) and line a baking sheet with parchment paper.
- In a medium saucepan, combine water, butter, and salt over medium heat.
- Bring the mixture to a boil, then reduce heat to low. Add the flour and stir vigorously until the dough forms a ball and pulls away from the sides of the pan.
- Remove from heat and allow the mixture to cool for 5 minutes.
- Beat in the eggs, one at a time, until the dough is smooth and glossy.
- Transfer the dough to a piping bag fitted with a round tip and pipe 3-inch strips onto the prepared baking sheet.
- Bake for 20–25 minutes or until golden brown and puffed. Allow to cool completely before filling.

2. Prepare the Matcha Honey Filling:
- In a mixing bowl, combine Greek yogurt, honey, and matcha powder. Whisk until smooth and creamy.
- Transfer the filling to a piping bag with a narrow tip.

3. Fill the Eclairs:
- Use a small knife to poke holes in the ends of each éclair.
- Pipe the matcha honey filling into the eclairs, ensuring they are evenly filled.

4. Add the Honey Glaze:
- Warm the honey slightly to make it more spreadable, then brush it over the top of each éclair.
- Dust lightly with matcha powder for a decorative finish.

5. Serve:
- Let the eclairs set for 10 minutes to allow the glaze to soak in. Serve fresh for the best flavor and texture.

HONEY ALMOND CRÈME BRÛLÉE

This elegant dessert is naturally sweetened with honey and made creamy with almond milk. It's a luxurious yet healthy treat that satisfies your sweet tooth without refined sugar.

Serves: 6
Prep Time: 15 minutes
Cook Time: 40 minutes

Ingredients

- 1 ½ cups unsweetened almond milk
- 4 large egg yolks
- 1/3 cup raw honey
- 1 teaspoon pure vanilla extract
- A pinch of sea salt
- 2 tablespoons coconut sugar (for caramelizing)

Instructions

1 Prepare the Mixture:
- Preheat your oven to 325°F (160°C).
- In a small saucepan, heat almond milk over medium heat until it begins to simmer. Remove from heat and let cool slightly.
- In a mixing bowl, whisk the egg yolks, honey, vanilla extract, and sea salt until well combined.

2 Combine and Strain:
- Slowly pour the warm almond milk into the egg mixture, whisking constantly to avoid cooking the eggs.
- Strain the mixture through a fine-mesh sieve into a clean bowl to remove any lumps.

3 Bake the Crème Brûlée:
- Divide the mixture evenly among six small ramekins.
- Place the ramekins in a baking dish and pour hot water into the dish, ensuring it reaches halfway up the sides of the ramekins.
- Bake for 35–40 minutes, or until the custard is set but still slightly jiggly in the center.
- Remove from the oven and let cool to room temperature, then refrigerate for at least 2 hours or overnight.

4 Caramelize the Top:
- Sprinkle 1 teaspoon of coconut sugar over each custard.
- Using a kitchen torch, caramelize the sugar until it melts and forms a golden, crispy layer. Let it cool for a minute before serving.

HONEY CINNAMON SWIRL BREAD PUDDING

This Honey Cinnamon Swirl Bread Pudding combines the warmth of cinnamon with the natural sweetness of honey for a comforting dessert. It's a healthier take on a classic recipe, packed with whole-grain bread, low-fat milk, and no refined sugar.

Serves: 6
Prep Time: 15 minutes
Cook Time: 35 minutes

Ingredients

- 6 cups whole-grain bread, cubed
- 3 large eggs
- 1 ½ cups unsweetened almond milk
- ½ cup honey
- 2 teaspoons ground cinnamon
- 1 teaspoon vanilla extract
- ¼ teaspoon salt
- ½ cup raisins (optional)
- 1 tablespoon melted butter (for greasing the baking dish)

Instructions

1 Prepare the Bread:
- Preheat your oven to 350°F (175°C).
- Grease a 9x9-inch baking dish with melted butter.
- Spread the cubed bread evenly in the baking dish.

2 Make the Custard:
- In a large mixing bowl, whisk together the eggs, almond milk, honey, cinnamon, vanilla extract, and salt until smooth.
- If using raisins, stir them into the mixture.

3 Combine and Bake:
- Pour the custard evenly over the bread cubes, ensuring all pieces are soaked.
- Gently press the bread down with a spatula to help absorb the custard.
- Let the mixture sit for 10 minutes to allow the bread to fully soak up the custard.

4 Bake:
- Place the baking dish in the preheated oven and bake for 35 minutes, or until the top is golden brown and the custard is set.

5 Serve:
- Let the bread pudding cool for 5–10 minutes before serving.
- Optionally, drizzle with additional honey or a dollop of Greek yogurt for extra flavor.

THANK YOU

Thank you for joining us on this delicious journey through 33 Super Healthy Honey Dessert Recipes! We hope these naturally sweetened treats have not only satisfied your sweet tooth but also inspired you to embrace the wholesome goodness of honey in your desserts.

Whether you're a seasoned baker or new to the kitchen, these recipes are designed to make healthy, delicious desserts accessible to everyone.

We'd love to see how you bring these recipes to life! Don't forget to follow us on Instagram at @health.base33 (https://instagram.com/health.base33) for more health tips, recipe inspiration, and community fun. Share your honey-infused creations with us by tagging @health.base33—you might even be featured on our page to inspire others! Your creativity helps build a supportive and vibrant community of dessert lovers who value health and flavor in every bite.

If you've enjoyed this book, we'd greatly appreciate it if you could leave a 5-star review on Amazon. Your feedback not only helps others discover these incredible recipes but also supports our mission of sharing healthy, honey-sweetened desserts with the world. Your review means the world to us and inspires us to keep creating more wholesome and delicious recipe collections.

Thank you for being a part of our honey-loving community. We can't wait to see your creations on Instagram and hear your feedback on Amazon. Here's to sweet, healthy treats and the joy they bring! Happy baking!

My Recipe

Recipe Name

Review ☆☆☆☆☆

Serving

_____

Prep Time

_____

Cook Time

_____

Ingredients

_____
_____
_____
_____
_____
_____
_____
_____

Directions

_____
_____
_____
_____
_____
_____

Notes

_____
_____
_____

☐ Vegetarian ☐ Vegan ☐ Dairy Free ☐ Gluten Free ☐ Low Carb

Printed in Dunstable, United Kingdom